Is It a Fi

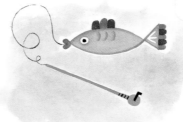

by Trent Brekard   illustrated by JoAnn Adinolfi

Orlando   Boston   Dallas   Chicago   San Diego

Visit *The Learning Site!*

www.harcourtschool.com

Requests for permission to make copies of any part of the work should be addressed to School Permissions and Copyrights, Harcourt, Inc., 6277 Sea Harbor Drive, Orlando, Florida 32887-6777. Fax: 407-345-2418.

HARCOURT and the Harcourt Logo are trademarks of Harcourt, Inc., registered in the United States of America and/or other jurisdictions.

Printed in China

ISBN 0-15-325435-1

8 9 10 121 10 09 08 07 06 05 04

Ordering Options
ISBN 0-15-323766-X (Collection)
ISBN 0-15-329607-0 (package of 5)

Here we are!
Get a rod.

Tug, tug, tug.
Is it a fish?
No, it is a man!

Tug, tug, tug.
Did Mom get a fish?
No, it is a bug!

Tug, tug, tug.
Is it a fish?
No, it is a hen!

Tug, tug, tug.
Did Ted get a fish?
No, it is a jug!

Tug, tug, tug.
Is it a fish?

Come look.
See what Jen got.
It is a big fish!